ITALIAN
COOKING

Photography by Peter Barry
Recipes styled by Jacqueline Bellefontaine
Designed by Richard Hawke and Claire Leighton
Edited by Jillian Stewart and Kate Cranshaw

3562
© 1994 Coombe Books
This edition published in 1994 by Coombe Books
for Parragon Book Service Ltd., Unit 13-17,
Avonbridge Trading Estate, Atlantic Road,
Avonbridge, Bath
All rights reserved.
Printed in Hong Kong
ISBN 1-85813-452-8

ITALIAN COOKING

PARRAGON

Contents

Introduction

Whenever you ask someone about Italian food they immediately think of pasta and pizza. Immortalised in restaurants all over the world, they are undoubtedly Italy's most famous food exports. Yet Italian cuisine has much to offer besides these undeniably delicious treats.

The great strength of Italian cuisine is its regional diversity and its reliance on fresh, locally available produce. Thanks to its favourable geography and climate, Italy has an abundance of fresh produce, from vegetables and fruit to cheeses and seafood. Italian cooking does not, therefore, rely on expensive ingredients or complex techniques, but rather on making the best of natural, good-quality produce. In Sicily, for example, salads and vegetable dishes based on locally grown artichokes are common, as are veal and chicken dishes using Marsala, the sweet fortified wine made on the island. Each area of Italy has its own speciality: Rome is justly famous for cheeses such as Mozzarella and Ricotta, Apulia is renowned for its seafood, and Naples has the honour of producing some of the world's most delicious ice creams.

With such a wonderful culinary tradition, it is obvious that food is important to Italians. Meal times are an opportunity for the family to get together, to relax, to chat, and most of all to enjoy a leisurely meal. The food is usually accompanied with local Italian wines or mineral water. The menu may include soup, antipasto, pasta, risotto, or possibly a meat dish (often veal or chicken), with a variety of vegetables or a salad. The Italian climate means a long growing season, so fruit trees flourish, as do grape vines. With fresh local melons, figs, grapes, peaches and pears widely available, it is little wonder that Italians often finish off a meal with fruit. Desserts such as ice cream and cakes tend to be reserved for special occasions, or are enjoyed in the many coffee houses so popular in Italian towns.

Whether it's a mouthwatering ice cream, a traditional pasta bake or a stylish seafood dish, Italian cooking is a celebration of the best food the land has to offer and the enthusiasm of the cook who prepares it. So why not bring a taste of Italy into your kitchen and discover cooking Italian style – it's simpler and more enjoyable than you ever imagined!

MINESTRONE

Everyone's favourite Italian soup doesn't always have to contain pasta. Our's substitutes potatoes and is hearty enough to serve as a meal.

SERVES 8-10

225g/8oz dried white cannellini beans
2 tbsps olive oil
1 large ham bone, preferably prosciutto
1 onion, chopped
2 cloves garlic, crushed
4 sticks celery, sliced
2 carrots, diced
1 small head Savoy cabbage or 460g/1lb
    fresh spinach, well washed
120g/4oz French beans, cut into 2.5cm/
    1-inch lengths
225g/8oz tomatoes, peeled, seeded and
    diced
1 dried red chilli
2.8 litres/5 pints water (or half beef stock)
1 sprig fresh rosemary
1 bay leaf
3 potatoes, peeled and cut into small dice
3 courgettes, trimmed and cut into small
    dice
1 tbsp chopped fresh basil
1 tbsp chopped fresh parsley
Grated Parmesan cheese

1. Place the beans in a large bowl, cover with cold water and leave to soak overnight.

2. Heat the oil in a large stock pot and add ham bone, onion and garlic. Cook until the onion has softened but not coloured. Add the celery, carrots, cabbage and green beans. If using spinach, reserve until later.

3. Drain the beans and add them to the pot with the tomatoes and the chilli. Add the water and bring to the boil, skimming the surface as necessary. Add the rosemary and bay leaf and simmer, uncovered, for about 1¼ hours, or until the beans are tender.

4. Add the potatoes and cook for a further 20 minutes.

5. Add the courgettes and spinach, if using, and cook, skimming the surface, for about 20 minutes longer. Remove the ham bone, rosemary and bay leaf and add basil and parsley and adjust the seasoning. Serve with Parmesan cheese.

TIME: Preparation takes about 20 minutes plus overnight soaking for the beans. Cooking takes about 2 hours.

SERVING IDEA: If wished, cooked pasta may be substituted for the potatoes and added at the end of cooking time.

VARIATION: Other varieties of dried white beans or canned beans may also be used. If using canned beans, add them with courgettes and spinach. Other vegetables such as broccoli, turnips, leeks or quartered Brussels sprouts, may be substituted.

TOMATO SOUP

Horseradish adds a bit of kick to this soup. Use fresh plum tomatoes if available.

SERVES 4

30g/1oz butter or margarine
1 small onion, chopped
1 small green pepper, chopped
1 tbsp flour
1 litre/1¾ pints brown stock, or water plus 2
    beef stock cubes
460g/1lb tomatoes, chopped
2 tbsps tomato purée
Salt and pepper
1 tbsp grated horseradish
120g/4oz short-cut/elbow macaroni
2 tbsps soured cream, to garnish
1 tbsp chopped parsley, to garnish

1. Heat the butter in a pan, add the onion and green pepper, cover and cook for 5 minutes.

2. Add the flour and stir. Add the stock gradually, then the tomatoes and tomato purée. Simmer for 15 minutes.

3. Purée the soup and strain. Return to the pan, and season with salt and pepper to taste.

4. Add the macaroni about 10-12 minutes before serving. Simmer and stir occasionally.

5. Add the horseradish just before serving, then garnish with the soured cream and parsley and serve immediately.

TIME: Preparation takes about 15 minutes and cooking takes about 30 minutes.

SERVING IDEA: Serve with crusty bread.

VARIATION: Use soup pasta such as extra small stellette (stars) or conchigliette piccole (tiny shells) instead of macaroni.

Anchovy Pâté with Crudités

This pâté is extremely quick to prepare and makes an excellent starter for a dinner party or alternatively, serve as a snack with drinks.

SERVES 4

Pâté

225g/8oz canned anchovies
60ml/4 tbsps olive oil
60g/2oz Bel Paese
90g/3oz pitted black olives
2 tbsps capers
1 tbsp Dijon mustard
1 tsp ground pepper

Crudités

Cucumber
Celery
Carrots
Spring onions
Radishes
Red and yellow peppers
Cauliflower
Mushrooms
Tomatoes
French beans
Mange tout

1. Put all ingredients for the pâté into the bowl of a blender or food processor and run the machine until well mixed. The mixture may have to be worked in 2 batches.

2. Chose a selection of crudités to serve with the pâté and prepare accordingly.

3. Cut cucumber, celery and carrots into batons. Trim spring onions and radishes. Slice peppers lengthways into strips.

4. Divide cauliflower into small florets. Leave small button mushrooms and cherry tomatoes whole, or quarter large ones.

5. Blanch trimmed French beans and mange tout in boiling water for about ½-1 minute or until bright green. Drain immediately and refresh in cold water.

TIME: Preparation takes 15 minutes.

SERVING IDEA: Serve the pâté in a bowl set on a large plate. Surround the pâté with the chosen vegetables, or accompany with Italian bread or toast.

SPINACH GNOCCHI

Gnocchi are dumplings that are served like pasta. A dish of gnocchi can be served as a first course or as a light main course, sprinkled with cheese or accompanied by a sauce.

SERVES 4-6

120g/4oz chopped, frozen spinach
225g/8oz ricotta cheese
90g/3oz Parmesan cheese
Salt and pepper
Freshly grated nutmeg
1 egg, slightly beaten
Butter

1. Defrost the spinach and press it between two plates to extract all the moisture.

2. Mix the spinach with the ricotta cheese, half the Parmesan cheese, salt, pepper and nutmeg. Gradually add the egg, beating well until the mixture holds together when shaped.

3. With floured hands, shape the mixture into ovals. Use about 1 tbsp of mixture for each gnocchi.

4. Lower 3 or 4 at a time into simmering water and allow to cook gently for about 1-2 minutes or until the gnocchi float to the surface.

5. Remove with a slotted spoon and place in a well buttered ovenproof dish.

6. When all the gnocchi are cooked, sprinkle on the remaining Parmesan cheese and dot with butter.

7. Reheat for 10 minutes in a hot oven and brown under a pre-heated grill before serving.

TIME: Preparation takes about 15 minutes, cooking takes about 20 minutes.

SERVING IDEA: Accompany with a tomato or cheese sauce and a salad or hot bread for a light meal.

COOK'S TIP: Gnocchi are best served soon after they are cooked. If allowed to stand overnight they become very heavy.

MUSSELS ALLA GENOVESE

These mussels make a very attractive starter for a special occasion.

SERVES 2

570ml/1 pint live mussels
Flour or oatmeal
1 shallot, finely chopped
Lemon juice
1 small handful fresh basil leaves
1 handful parsley
1 clove garlic, chopped
15g/½oz walnut halves, chopped
1 tbsp freshly grated Parmesan
Salt and pepper
15g/1oz butter
2-3 tbsps olive oil
Fresh bay leaves or basil leaves

1. Scrub the mussels well and discard any with broken shells or those that will not close. Put the mussels into a bowl of clean water with a handful of flour or oatmeal. Leave for ½ hour, then rinse under clear water.

2. Put the shallot into a large saucepan with some lemon juice, and cook for a few minutes, until the shallot softens.

3. Add the mussels and a pinch of salt and pepper. Cover the pan and cook the mussels quickly for 4-5 minutes, shaking the pan.

4. When the mussel shells have opened, take the mussels out of the pan, set aside and keep warm. Strain the cooking liquid for possible use later.

5. To prepare the Genovese sauce, put the herbs, garlic, nuts, 1 tbsp grated cheese and salt and pepper into a food processor and work to chop roughly. Add butter and work again.

6. With the machine running, add the oil gradually through the feed tube. If the sauce is still too thick, add the reserved liquid from cooking the mussels.

7. Remove the top shells from mussels and discard. Arrange the mussels evenly in 2 shallow dishes, spoon some of the sauce into each. Sprinkle the top lightly with remaining Parmesan cheese and garnish with bay or basil leaves to serve.

TIME: Preparation takes 15 minutes and cooking takes 6-8 minutes.
PREPARATION: Prepare the sauce in advance if wished.
SERVING IDEA: Serve with bread and butter triangles.

BRUSCHETTA WITH TOMATOES

Cooked over a wood fire in the traditional way, or more conveniently in the oven, tomatoes, basil and crisp bread make an unusual and informal starter.

SERVES 6-8

18 slices of crusty Italian bread, cut
    2.5cm/1-inch thick
2 cloves garlic, crushed
140ml/¼ pint olive oil
Salt and pepper
4-5 ripe tomatoes, depending on size
18 large fresh basil leaves

1. Place the bread slices on a baking sheet and toast for about 10 minutes on each side in a preheated oven, at 190°C/375°F/Gas Mark 5.

2. Spread some of the garlic on both sides of each slice.

3. Heat the oil gently in a small saucepan. Arrange the bread on a serving plate and immediately pour over the warm oil. Sprinkle with salt and pepper.

4. Slice the tomatoes in 1.25cm/½-inch rounds. Place one basil leaf and one slice of tomato on each slice of bread and serve immediately.

TIME: Preparation takes about 15 minutes, cooking time about 25 minutes.

VARIATIONS: French bread may be used if Italian bread is not available, but the flavour will be different. White or brown bread may be used.

SERVING IDEA: May be served as a first course or as cocktail savouries.

MELON AND PROSCIUTTO

This is one of the best-loved Italian starters. It deserves to be, because the flavour of a ripe melon and the richness of Italian ham complement one another perfectly.

SERVES 4

1 large ripe melon
16 thin slices prosciutto ham

1. Cut the melon in half lengthways, scoop out the seeds and discard them.

2. Cut the melon into quarters and carefully pare off the rind. Cut each quarter lengthways into four slices.

3. Wrap each slice of melon in a slice of prosciutto and place on a serving dish. Alternatively, place the melon slices on the dish and cover with the slices of prosciutto, leaving the ends of the melon showing. Serve immediately.

TIME: Preparation takes about 15-20 minutes.

VARIATIONS: Place the slices of prosciutto flat on serving plates or roll them up into cigar shapes. Serve with quartered fresh figs instead of melon.

PASTA SHELLS WITH SEAFOOD

Prawns and scallops in a creamy white wine sauce make a wonderful combination with pasta.

SERVES 4

60g/2oz butter or margarine
2 cloves garlic, crushed
120ml/4 fl oz dry white wine
225ml/8 fl oz double cream
1 tbsp cornflour
2 tbsps water
1 tbsp lemon juice
Salt and pepper
225g/8oz pasta shells
460g/1lb prawns, peeled and de-veined
120g/4oz scallops, cleaned and sliced
1 tbsp chopped parsley

1. Melt the butter in a pan. Add the garlic, and cook for 1 minute. Add the wine and cream, bring back to boil and cook for 2 minutes.

2. Slake the cornflour with the water, and pour into sauce. Stir until boiling. Add the lemon juice and salt and pepper to taste.

3. Meanwhile, cook the pasta in plenty of boiling salted water, for about 10 minutes or until 'al dente'. Drain, shaking to remove the excess water.

4. Add the prawns and scallops to sauce and cook for 3 minutes. Pour over the pasta shells, toss, and garnish with the parsley.

TIME: Preparation takes 5 minutes and cooking takes about 15 minutes.

SERVING IDEA: Serve as a starter for 8 people.

FISH MILANESE

These fish, cooked in the style of Milan, have a crispy crumb coating and the fresh tang of lemon juice.

SERVES 4

8 small or 4 large sole or plaice fillets,
  skinned
2 tbsps dry vermouth
90ml/6 tbsps olive oil
1 bay leaf
Seasoned flour for dredging
2 eggs, lightly beaten
Dry breadcrumbs
Oil for shallow frying
90g/3oz butter
1 clove garlic, crushed
2 tsps chopped parsley
1 tsp chopped fresh oregano
2 tbsps capers
Juice of 1 lemon
Salt and pepper
Lemon wedges and parsley to garnish

1. Remove any small bones from the fish and place in a large, shallow dish. Combine the vermouth, oil and bay leaf in a small saucepan and heat gently. Allow to cool completely and pour over the fish. Leave the fish to marinate for about 1 hour, turning them occasionally.

2. Remove the fish from the marinade and dredge lightly with the seasoned flour.

3. Dip the fillets into the beaten eggs to coat, or use a pastry brush to brush the eggs onto the fillets. Dip the egg-coated fillet into the breadcrumbs, pressing the crumbs on firmly.

4. Heat the oil in a large frying pan. Add the fillets and cook slowly for about 3-4 minutes on each side, until golden brown, remove and drain on kitchen paper.

5. Pour the oil out of the frying pan and wipe it clean. Add the butter and the garlic and cook until both turn a light brown. Add the herbs, capers and lemon juice and pour immediately over the fish. Garnish with lemon wedges and sprigs of parsley.

TIME: Preparation takes 1 hour for the fish to marinate, cooking takes about 6 minutes. It may be necessary to cook the fish in several batches, depending upon the size of the frying pan.

COOK'S TIP: If necessary, keep the fish fillets warm by placing on a wire cooling rack covered with kitchen paper and place in a warm oven, leaving the door slightly ajar. Sprinkling the fish fillets lightly with salt as they drain on kitchen paper helps to remove some of the oil.

VARIATIONS: Other white fish fillets may be prepared in the same way. Choose fillets that are of even size so that they cook in the same length of time. Chopped onion may be substituted for the garlic, if wished.

RED MULLET WITH HERB & MUSHROOM SAUCE

This is a Mediterranean fish with a slight taste of prawns. It is often cooked with the liver left in – a delicacy.

SERVES 4

460g/1lb small mushrooms, left whole
1 clove garlic, finely chopped
3 tbsps olive oil
1 tbsp finely chopped parsley
2 tsps finely chopped basil
1 tsp finely chopped marjoram or sage
Juice of 1 lemon
60ml/4 tbsps dry white wine mixed with
   ½ tsp cornflour
Few drops anchovy essence
4 red mullet, each weighing about
   225g/8oz, gutted and scaled
2 tsps white breadcrumbs
2 tsps freshly grated Parmesan cheese

1. Combine the mushrooms, garlic and olive oil in a small frying pan. Cook over moderate heat for about 1 minute, until the garlic and mushrooms are slightly softened.

2. Add all the herbs, lemon juice and white wine and cornflour mixture. Bring to the boil, stirring and cook until thickened. Add anchovy essence to taste.

3. Place the fish head to tail in a shallow ovenproof dish that can be used for serving. The fish should fit snugly into the dish.

4. Pour the prepared sauce over the fish and sprinkle with the breadcrumbs and Parmesan cheese.

5. Cover the dish loosely with foil and cook in an oven preheated to 190°C/375°F/ Gas Mark 5, for about 20 minutes. Uncover for the last 5 minutes, if wished and raise the oven temperature slightly to lightly brown the fish.

TIME: Preparation takes about 30 minutes, cooking takes about 5 minutes for the sauce and 20 minutes for the fish.

PREPARATION: If the fish need to be scaled, use the blunt edge of a knife and scrape from the tail to the head. Rinse well and remove any loose scales.

VARIATIONS: Use other fish such as bream or sardines.

SWORDFISH KEBABS

Swordfish is one of the most commonly caught fish in Southern Italy and Sicily. It won't fall apart during cooking – a bonus when making kebabs.

SERVES 4-6

1kg/2¼lbs swordfish steaks
90ml/3 fl oz olive oil
1 tsp chopped oregano
1 tsp chopped marjoram
Juice and grated rind of ½ lemon
4 tomatoes, cut into thick slices
2 lemons, cut into thin slices
Salt and freshly ground pepper
Lemon slices and flat leaf parsley for
    garnish

1. Cut the swordfish steaks into 5cm/2-inch pieces.

2. Mix the olive oil, herbs, lemon juice and rind together and set it aside.

3. Thread the swordfish, tomato slices and lemon slices onto skewers, alternating the ingredients.

4. Brush the kebabs with the oil and lemon juice mixture and cook under a preheated grill for about 10 minutes, basting frequently with the lemon and oil.

5. Serve garnished with lemons and parsley.

TIME: Preparation takes about 15 minutes, cooking takes about 10 minutes.

VARIATIONS: Fresh tuna may be used instead of swordfish. Use cherry tomatoes instead of sliced tomatoes, if available.

SERVING IDEA: Accompany the kebabs with risotto and a green salad.

SEAFOOD TORTA

*A very stylish version of a fish flan, this makes a perfect accompaniment to an
Italian aperitif or serves as a light supper dish with a salad.*

SERVES 6-8

Pastry

225g/8oz plain flour, sifted
120g/4oz unsalted butter
Pinch salt
60ml/4 tbsps cold milk

Filling

120g/4oz white fish fillets (plaice, sole or
    cod)
140ml/¼ pint water
140ml/¼ pint white wine
Pinch flaked dried chillies
225g/8oz cooked prawns
120g/4oz dressed crab
30g/1oz butter
2 tbsps flour
1 clove garlic, crushed
2 egg yolks
140ml/¼ pint double cream
Chopped fresh parsley
Salt and pepper

1. To prepare the pastry, sift the flour into a
bowl or onto a work surface. Cut the butter
into small pieces and rub them into the
flour until the mixture resembles fine
breadcrumbs. Make a well in the flour, pour
in the milk and add the pinch of salt. Mix
with a fork, gradually incorporating the
butter and flour mixture from the sides until
all the ingredients are mixed. This may also
be done in a food processor.

2. Form the dough into a ball, wrap in
cling film and leave the dough in the
refrigerator for about 1 hour.

3. To prepare the filling, cook the fish
fillets in the water and wine with the dried
chilli flakes for about 10 minutes or until just
firm to the touch. When the fish is cooked,
remove it from the liquid and flake it into a
bowl with the prawns and the crabmeat.
Reserve the cooking liquid.

4. Melt the butter in a small saucepan and
stir in the flour. Gradually strain on the
cooking liquid from the fish, stirring
constantly until smooth. Add garlic, place
over high heat and bring to the boil stirring.
Lower the heat and allow to cook for 1
minute. Add to the fish in the bowl and set
aside to cool.

5. On a well-floured surface, roll out the
pastry and transfer it with a rolling pin to a
loose bottomed flan tin. Press the pastry
into the tin and cut off any excess. Prick the
pastry case lightly with a fork and chill for
30 minutes. Place a sheet of greaseproof
paper inside the case and fill with dried
beans or baking beans. Bake the pastry
case blind for 15 minutes in an oven
preheated to 190°C/375°F/Gas Mark 5.

6. While the pastry is baking, combine the
egg yolks, cream and parsley and stir into
the fish filling. Adjust the seasoning with
salt and pepper. When the pastry is ready,
remove the paper and beans and pour in
the filling.

7. Return the flan to the oven and bake for
a further 25 minutes. Allow to cool slightly
then remove from the tin. Transfer to a
serving dish and slice before serving.

FISH RAVIOLI

Making pasta is not half as difficult as you may think, and tastes delicious.

SERVES 4

Filling

225g/8oz sole fillets, or flounder, skinned
 and boned
1 slice of onion
1 slice of lemon
6 peppercorns
1 bay leaf
1 tbsp lemon juice
225ml/8 fl oz water
2 eggs, beaten
2 tbsps breadcrumbs
1 spring onion, finely chopped

Pasta Dough

175g/6oz strong plain flour
Pinch of salt
3 eggs

Lemon Sauce

30g/1oz butter or margarine
2 tbsps flour
225ml/8 fl oz strained cooking liquid from
 fish
2 tbsps double cream
Salt and pepper
2 tbsps lemon juice

---

1. To make the filling, place the fish in an oven-proof dish with the slice of onion, slice of lemon, peppercorns, bay leaf, lemon juice and water. Cover and bake for 20 minutes in an oven preheated to 180°C/350°F/Gas Mark 4.

2. Remove the fish from the liquid, and allow to drain. Strain the liquid, and set aside. When the fish is cool, beat until smooth. Mix in the rest of the filling ingredients and season.

3. To make the dough, sift the flour and salt into a bowl, make a well in the centre and add the eggs. Work the flour and eggs together with a spoon, and then knead by hand, until a smooth dough is formed. Leave to rest for 15 minutes.

4. Lightly flour a pastry board, and roll out the dough thinly into a rectangle. Cut the dough in half.

5. Shape the filling into small balls, and set them about 4cm/1½-inch apart on one half of the dough. Place the other half on top, and cut with a ravioli cutter or small pastry cutter, seal the edges of each parcel.

6. Cook in batches in a large, wide pan with plenty of boiling salted water for about 8 minutes or until tender. Remove carefully with a slotted spoon.

7. Meanwhile, make the sauce by melting the butter in a pan. Stir in the flour, and cook for 30 seconds. Draw off the heat, and gradually stir in the liquid from cooked fish. Return to the heat and bring to the boil. Simmer for 4 minutes, stirring continuously.

8. Add the cream and mix well. Season to taste. Remove from the heat, and gradually stir in the lemon juice. Do not reboil. Pour the sauce over the ravioli and serve immediately.

TIME: Preparation takes about 30 minutes plus 15 minutes standing time.
Cooking takes about 40 minutes.

PEPPER SALAD WITH CAPERS

Capers, the flower buds of a plant that flourishes in the warm Italian climate, are a favourite ingredient in Italian cooking.

SERVES 4-6

3 large peppers, red, green and yellow
90ml/3 fl oz olive oil
1 clove garlic, finely chopped
Basil leaves, roughly chopped
Fresh marjoram roughly chopped
2 tbsps capers
1 tbsp white wine vinegar

1. Cut the peppers in half and remove the core and seeds. Press with the palm of the hand or the back of a knife to flatten. Brush the skin side with oil and place the peppers under a preheated grill.

2. Grill the peppers until the skins are well charred. Wrap in a towel and leave for 15 minutes. Unwrap and peel off the charred skin.

3. Cut the peppers into thick strips and arrange on a serving dish. Scatter over the chopped garlic, basil leaves, marjoram and capers.

4. Mix together the remaining olive oil with the vinegar and salt and pepper and pour over the salad. Refrigerate for 1 hour before serving.

TIME: Preparation takes about 30 minutes plus 1 hour refrigeration.

PREPARATION: The peppers may also be roasted in a hot oven for about 30 minutes. Alternatively, pierce whole peppers with a fork and hold them over a gas flame to char the skin.

WATCHPOINT: The peppers must become very charred on the outside before the skin will peel well.

COOK'S TIP: Instead of chopping them, the basil leaves may be rolled up and cut into strips with kitchen scissors.

VARIATION: The salad may be prepared with all red or all yellow peppers instead of the combination of the three colours. If using only red peppers, substitute red wine vinegar.

CHICKEN SALAD WITH PASTA SHELLS

This salad can be served as a side dish, a light meal or a main course salad.

SERVES 2-4

150g/5oz soup pasta shells (conchigliette piccole)
225g/8oz cooked chicken, shredded
200g/7oz can sweetcorn, drained
1 stick celery, sliced
1 red pepper, diced
1 green pepper, diced

Dressing
1 tbsp mayonnaise
2 tbsps vinegar
Salt and pepper

1. Cook the pasta in plenty of boiling, salted water until just tender. Drain well, and leave to cool.

2. Meanwhile, make the dressing. Combine the mayonnaise with the vinegar and salt and pepper to taste.

3. When the pasta is cool, add the shredded chicken, sweetcorn, celery and peppers. Toss well and serve with the dressing.

TIME: Preparation takes about 10 minutes and cooking takes about 10 minutes.

VARIATION: Add some chopped fresh herbs such as basil, parsley or tarragon and a little crushed garlic to the dressing.

STUFFED AUBERGINE

Aubergine stuffed with bacon, peppers and pasta in a tomato sauce, topped with cheese and breadcrumbs, makes an unusual main course dish.

SERVES 4

90g/3oz macaroni
4 small or 2 large aubergines
30g/1oz butter
1 small onion, chopped
1 clove garlic, crushed
225g/8oz bacon, diced
1 green pepper, diced
1 yellow pepper, diced
2 tomatoes, skinned, chopped and seeded
1 tbsp tomato purée
½ tsp chilli powder
Salt and pepper
30g/1oz Mozzarella cheese, grated
1 tbsp breadcrumbs

1. Cook the macaroni in plenty of boiling, salted water for 10 minutes, or until 'al dente'. Rinse in cold water, and drain well.

2. Wrap the aubergines in foil, and bake in an oven preheated to 180°C/350°F/Gas Mark 4 for 30 minutes.

3. Cut the aubergines in half, lengthwise. Scoop out the flesh, leaving a 1.5cm/½-inch thickness on the skin. Chop the flesh.

4. Heat the butter in a pan. Add the onion and garlic, and cook until transparent. Add the bacon and peppers and sauté for 5 minutes.

5. Add the chopped aubergine, tomatoes, tomato purée, chilli powder, and salt and pepper and cook for a further 3 minutes.

6. Stir in the macaroni, and fill the scooped-out aubergine halves with the mixture.

7. Top with the grated cheese and breadcrumbs, and brown under a hot grill or in a preheated oven at 200°C/400°F/Gas Mark 6. Serve immediately.

TIME: Preparation takes about 15 minutes and cooking takes about 50-55 minutes.

SERVING IDEA: Serve with rice and a mixed green salad.

SALAD OF PASTA QUILLS

Pasta makes a great base for a salad, and is a good way of using up leftover cooked pasta too.

SERVES 4

175g/6oz penne
1 × 185g/6½oz can tuna, drained and flaked
3 tomatoes, quartered
½ cucumber, cut into batons
120g/4oz green beans, cooked
12 black olives, halved and pitted
6-8 anchovy fillets, drained, and soaked in milk if wished
120ml/4 fl oz ready-made vinaigrette dressing

1. Cook the penne in lots of boiling salted water until 'al dente'. Rinse in cold water; drain, and leave to dry.

2. Put the flaked tuna in the base of a salad dish. Toss the pasta together with tomatoes, cucumber, green beans, olives, and anchovies, then pour over the oil and vinegar dressing. Mix together well.

TIME: Preparation takes 15 minutes, cooking takes about 12 minutes.

COOK'S TIP: Soaking the anchovy fillets in milk takes away some of the saltiness.

ROMAN-STYLE ARTICHOKES

Artichoke hearts coated in a basil-flavoured tomato sauce and sprinkled with Parmesan cheese.

SERVES 4

Juice of 2 lemons

16 small artichokes

1 tbsp chopped chives

4 large tomatoes, peeled, seeded and roughly chopped

2 tbsps olive oil

5 fresh basil leaves, chopped

Salt and pepper

30g/4 tbsps grated Parmesan cheese

---

1. Fill a bowl with water and add the lemon juice.

2. Cut the hard stalk ends off of the artichokes and, using a small, sharp knife, cut off all the leaves, leaving the hearts whole.

3. Place the artichoke hearts in the bowl of lemon water as soon as the leaves are removed, to prevent discolouration.

4. Cook the artichoke hearts in salted, boiling water until tender, testing them after about 15 minutes with the point of a sharp knife.

5. Mix together the chives, tomato, 1 tbsp olive oil, basil and plenty of salt and pepper.

6. Remove the choke from each artichoke heart. Grease an ovenproof dish with the remaining oil and place the hearts in the dish.

7. Spoon the tomato sauce onto each heart, sprinkle over the Parmesan cheese and crisp up in a hot oven. Serve hot.

TIME: Preparation takes about 20 minutes and cooking takes 30-40 minutes.

VARIATION: Use 4 large artichokes instead of small ones.

COOK'S TIP: Use a very sharp knife to cut off the leaves as they are very hard.

FLAGEOLET, TUNA AND TOMATO SALAD

Tuna and tomatoes are two popular ingredients in Italian antipasto dishes. Add beans, with their pale green colour, for an attractive and easy salad or starter.

SERVES 6-8

460g/1lb canned flageolet beans (substitute
    white haricot beans or butter beans)
175g/6oz canned tuna in oil
Chopped fresh herbs (parsley, oregano,
    basil or marjoram)
Juice of 1 lemon
120ml/4 fl oz olive oil
Salt and pepper
6-8 tomatoes

1. Drain the beans, rinse and leave in a colander to dry. Drain the tuna and flake it into a bowl.

2. Chop the herbs finely and mix with the lemon juice, oil, salt and pepper. Add the beans to the tuna fish in the bowl and pour over the dressing, tossing carefully. Do not allow the tuna to break up too much.

3. Adjust the seasoning and pile the salad into a mound in a shallow serving dish. Cut the tomatoes into rounds about 5mm/ ¼-inch thick and place against the mound of salad. Serve immediately.

TIME: Preparation takes about 15 minutes.

SERVING IDEA: If wished, serve the salad on individual plates lined with radicchio or curly endive.

VARIATIONS: Add chopped spring onions or red onions to the salad or add finely chopped garlic.

SICILIAN CAPONATA

Vegetables, so important in Italian cuisine, are often served separately. This combination makes an excellent vegetable course, accompaniment or starter.

SERVES 6

1 aubergine
Salt
140ml/¼ pint olive oil
1 onion, sliced
2 red peppers, cut into 2.5cm/1-inch pieces
2 sticks celery, sliced thickly
460g/1lb canned plum tomatoes
2 tbsps red wine vinegar
1 tbsp sugar
1 clove garlic, crushed
Salt and pepper
12 black olives
1 tbsp capers

1. Cut the aubergine in half and score the cut surface. Sprinkle with salt and leave to drain in a colander or on kitchen paper for 30 minutes. Rinse, pat dry and cut into 2.5cm/1-inch cubes.

2. Heat the oil in a large frying pan and add the onion, peppers and celery. Lower the heat and cook for about 5 minutes, stirring occasionally. Add the aubergine and cook a further 5 minutes.

3. Sieve the tomatoes to remove the seeds and add the pulp and liquid to the vegetables in the frying pan. Add the remaining ingredients except the olives and capers and cook for a further 2 minutes.

4. To remove the stones from the olives, roll them on a flat surface to loosen the stones and then remove them with a vegetable peeler or a cherry pitter. Slice the olives into quarters and add to the vegetables with the capers.

5. Simmer, uncovered, over a moderate heat for 15 minutes to evaporate most of the liquid. Adjust the seasoning and serve hot or cold.

TIME: Preparation takes 35 minutes including standing time and cooking takes about 30 minutes.

COOK'S TIP: When serving cold, caponata may be prepared two days in advance.

TOMATO SALAD RUSTICA

An informal salad with a country flavour, this is perfect with barbecued meat, poultry or fish.

SERVES 4

4-6 canned anchovy fillets
Milk
460g/1lb tomatoes
1 onion
2 tbsps capers
1 tsp chopped fresh oregano or basil
Salt and pepper
90ml/3 fl oz olive oil
1 tbsp lemon juice

1. Soak the anchovies in a little milk before using, rinse and pat dry. Cut the tomatoes into quarters and remove the cores. Slice each quarter in half again and place them in a serving bowl.

2. Slice the onion into thin rounds and then separate into rings. Scatter over the tomatoes. Cut the anchovies into small pieces and add to the tomatoes and onions along with the capers.

3. Mix the herbs, salt and pepper, oil and lemon juice together until well emulsified and pour over the salad. Mix all the ingredients gently and leave to stand for about 30 minutes before serving.

TIME: Preparation takes about 20 minutes. Salad must stand for 30 minutes before serving.

COOK'S TIP: Soaking the anchovies in milk removes some of the strong taste and saltiness of the fish.

SERVING IDEA: Serve as a side dish, or with a combination of other salads in an antipasti selection.

VARIATIONS: Use red onions or spring onions for a change. Add sliced black olives if wished.

LASAGNE

Strips of home-made pasta, cooked with beef, onion, mushrooms, wine and tomato make for a very filling dish.

SERVES 4

Pasta Dough
400g/14oz flour, sifted
Salt
3 eggs, beaten

Lasagne Filling
60g/2oz butter
1 medium onion, chopped
1 clove garlic, chopped
600g/1lb 5oz minced beef
2 mushrooms, rinsed and chopped
60ml/2 fl oz white wine
520ml/18 fl oz chicken stock
Sprig of thyme
1 bay leaf
1 tbsp tomato purée
Salt and pepper
30g/4 tbsps grated Parmesan cheese

1. To make the dough, sift the flour and salt in a mixing bowl. Make a well in the centre and add the eggs. Work the flour and eggs together with a spoon, then knead by hand until a smooth dough is formed. Cover and refrigerate for 30 minutes.

2. Heat half of the butter in a frying pan and cook the onion and garlic until light brown.

3. Stir in the meat and mushrooms and cook for 2 minutes or until the meat is browned.

4. Deglaze the pan with the white wine, allow it to reduce and stir in 275ml/10 fl oz of the chicken stock. Add the thyme, bay leaf and tomato purée, season with salt and pepper and cook until the liquid has reduced by half. Remove the thyme and bay leaf.

5. Roll the dough out thinly or pass it through a pasta machine and cut into even-sized rectangular strips.

6. Cook the pasta strips for 1 minute in salted, boiling water, rinse under hot water and set aside to drain on a slightly damp tea towel.

7. Grease an ovenproof dish with the remaining butter and lay strips of pasta into the base.

8. Cover each layer of pasta with a layer of the meat sauce and continue layering until all the pasta and sauce has been used up.

9. Pour over the remaining chicken stock, sprinkle over the grated Parmesan cheese and cook in a preheated oven at 200°C/400°F/Gas Mark 6 for about 40 minutes, or until the juices have almost entirely evaporated. Serve piping hot from the oven.

TIME: Preparation takes about 45 minutes and cooking takes approximately 50 minutes.

COOK'S TIP: The pasta should be rolled out thin enough so that you can see through it. If using a pasta machine, follow manufacturers instructions.

ITALIAN CASSEROLE

Serve this hearty dish with a mixed leaf salad.

SERVES 4

120g/4oz small macaroni
30g/1oz butter or margarine
1 onion, chopped
1 clove garlic, crushed
1 × 460g/1lb can plum tomatoes
1 tbsp tomato purée
1 red pepper, roughly chopped
1 green pepper, roughly chopped
225g/8oz salami, cut into chunks
10 black olives, halfed, and pitted
Salt and pepper
120g/4oz Mozzarella cheese, sliced thinly

1. Cook the macaroni in plenty of boiling salted water for 10 minutes, or until 'al dente'.

2. Rinse under hot water and drain well. Place in a shallow, oven-proof dish.

3. Meanwhile, heat the butter in pan, and sauté onion and garlic gently until soft.

4. Add the undrained tomatoes, tomato purée, red and green peppers, salami and olives, and stir well. Simmer uncovered for 5 minutes. Season with salt and pepper.

5. Pour over the macaroni, stir, and cover with the sliced cheese.

6. Bake uncovered in an oven preheated to 180°C/350°F/Gas Mark 4, for 20 minutes, until cheese has melted. Serve immediately.

TIME: Preparation takes about 15 minutes and cooking takes about 35 minutes.

VARIATION: If wished, omit the salami and add other vegetables, such as courgettes, to the tomato sauce to make a vegetarian meal.

MACARONI CHEESE WITH ANCHOVIES

*As macaroni cheese is a meal that can be made and on the table in 20 minutes,
keep the ingredients in stock to feed unexpected guests in a hurry.*

SERVES 4

6-8 canned anchovy fillets
225g/8oz macaroni
60g/2oz butter or margarine
3 tbsps flour
430ml/¾ pint milk
½ tsp dry mustard
90g/3oz Fontina cheese, grated
Salt and pepper

1. Drain the anchovies, and set enough aside to slice to make a thin lattice over the dish. Chop the rest finely.

2. Cook the macaroni in plenty of boiling salted water for 10 minutes, or until 'al dente'. Rinse in hot water and drain well.

3. Meanwhile, melt the butter in a pan. Stir in the flour and cook for 1 minute. Remove from the heat, and gradually stir in the milk.

4. Return to the heat and bring to the boil. Simmer for 3 minutes, stirring occasionally.

5. Stir in the mustard, anchovies, and half the cheese. Season with salt and pepper to taste. Stir in the macaroni, and pour into an oven-proof dish.

6. Sprinkle the remaining cheese over the top, and make a latticework with the remaining anchovies. Brown under a hot grill. Serve immediately.

TIME: Preparation takes 5 minutes and cooking takes 12-14 minutes.

COOK'S TIP: Add a few chopped fresh herbs such as parsley or basil to the sauce.

PIZZA WITH PEPPERS, OLIVES & ANCHOVIES

Pizza really needs no introduction. It originated in Naples and has been adopted everywhere. Change the toppings to suit your taste.

SERVES 4

Pizza Dough

15g/½oz fresh yeast
½ tsp sugar
175ml/6 fl oz lukewarm water
225g/8oz plain flour
Pinch salt
2 tbsps oil

Tomato Sauce

2 tsps olive oil
1 onion, finely chopped
1 clove garlic, crushed
1 × 460g/1lb can tomatoes
1 tbsp tomato purée
½ tsp each oregano and basil
1 tsp sugar
Salt and pepper

Topping

120g/4oz mozzarella cheese, grated
2 tbsps grated Parmesan cheese
½ red pepper, sliced
½ green pepper, sliced
60g/2oz black olives, pitted
60g/2oz canned anchovies, drained

1. Cream the yeast with the sugar in a small bowl, add the lukewarm water and leave to stand for 10 minutes to work. Bubbles will appear on the surface when ready.

2. Sift flour and salt into a bowl, make a well in the centre, add the oil and the yeast mixture. Using a wooden spoon, beat the liquid in the centre of the well, gradually incorporating the flour from the outside until it forms a firm dough.

3. Turn the dough out onto a floured surface and knead for 10 minutes or until the dough is smooth and elastic. Place in a lightly oiled bowl or in a large plastic bag, cover or tie the bag and leave to stand in a warm place for 30 minutes, or until the dough has doubled in bulk.

4. Knock the dough back and knead it into a smooth ball. Flatten the dough and roll out on a floured surface into a 25cm/10-inch diameter circle.

5. To prepare the tomato sauce, heat the oil in a heavy-based saucepan and add the onion and the garlic. Cook until the onion and garlic have softened but not coloured. Add the tomatoes and their juice, tomato purée, herbs, sugar and salt and pepper.

6. Bring the sauce to the boil and then allow to simmer, uncovered, to reduce. Stir the sauce occasionally to prevent sticking. When the sauce is thick and smooth, leave it to cool.

7. Spread the cooled sauce over the pizza dough. Sprinkle half the cheese on top of the tomato sauce and then arrange the topping ingredients. Sprinkle with remaining cheese and bake in a preheated 200°C/400°F/Gas Mark 6 oven for 15-20 minutes or until the cheese is melted and bubbling and the crust is brown.

PASTA WITH CLAMS

This pasta dish is served simply with clams, butter and garlic.

SERVES 4

460g/1lb clams
120ml/4 fl oz white wine
1 shallot, chopped
300g/11oz fresh pasta
60g/2oz butter
1 clove garlic, chopped
½ tbsp chopped parsley
Salt and pepper

1. Place the clams in a large saucepan, pour in the white wine, add the shallot and place over a high heat. Shake the saucepan frequently until the clams open. Remove from the heat and set the pan aside until the clams are cool enough to handle.

2. Remove the clams from their shells.

3. Cook the pasta to your liking in salted, boiling water. Rinse in hot water and set aside to drain.

4. Melt the butter in a saucepan, add the garlic, chopped parsley, pasta and the clams. Season with salt and pepper.

5. Keep on the heat, stirring well until the pasta is heated through. Serve immediately.

TIME: Preparation takes about 10 minutes and cooking takes approximately 20 minutes.

VARIATION: Other shellfish, such as whelks or cockles, may be added to this dish.

COOK'S TIP: When the clams are cooked and cooled, you can remove them from their shells, but keep them in the cooking juice until needed; this prevents them from drying out.

CANNELLONI

*Cannelloni, though quite lengthy to prepare, makes a delicious
and satisfying dish.*

SERVES 4

---

12 cannelloni tubes
2 tbsps Parmesan cheese, grated

Filling
1 tbsp olive oil
2 cloves garlic, crushed
1 onion, chopped
460g/1lb minced beef
1 tsp tomato purée
½ tsp basil
½ tsp oregano
225g/8oz chopped, cooked spinach
1 egg, lightly beaten
60ml/4 tbsps cream
Salt and pepper to taste

Tomato Sauce
1 tbsp olive oil
1 onion, chopped
1 clove garlic, crushed
1 × 400g/14oz can chopped tomatoes
2 tbsps tomato purée
Salt and pepper

Cream Sauce
225ml/8 fl oz milk
1 slice of onion
3 peppercorns
1 small bay leaf
30g/1oz butter or margarine
2 tbsps flour
Salt and pepper

---

1. To make the filling, heat the oil in a large frying pan and sauté the garlic and onion gently until soft and transparent. Add the meat and cook, stirring continuously, until well browned.

2. Drain off any fat, add the tomato purée, basil and oregano, and cook gently for 15 minutes.

3. Add the spinach, egg and cream, and salt and pepper to taste.

4. Cook the cannelloni in a large pan of boiling salted water for 15-20 minutes, until tender. Rinse in hot water and drain.

5. Fill carefully with the meat mixture, using a piping bag with a wide, plain nozzle, or a teaspoon.

6. To make the tomato sauce, heat the oil in a pan, add the onion and garlic, and cook gently until transparent.

7. Add the chopped tomatoes to the pan with the tomato purée and salt and pepper to taste. Bring to boil, and then simmer for 15-20 minutes until thickened to a sauce. Set aside.

8. To make the cream sauce, put the milk in a small saucepan with the onion, peppercorns and bay leaf. Heat gently for 1 minute, taking care not to boil, and set aside to cool for 5 minutes. Strain.

9. Melt the butter in a saucepan. Remove from the heat and stir in the flour. Gradually add the cool milk, and bring to the boil, stirring continuously, until the sauce thickens. Add seasoning to taste.

10. Spread the tomato sauce on the base of an ovenproof dish. Lay the cannelloni on top, and cover with the cream sauce.

11. Sprinkle with the grated cheese, and bake in an oven preheated to 180°C/350°F/ Gas Mark 4, for 30 minutes. Serve immediately.

SPAGHETTI CARBONARA

Spaghetti served in a rich sauce of cream, egg yolks, bacon and capers.

SERVES 4

460g/1lb spaghetti
60ml/2 fl oz milk
150ml/5 fl oz single cream
Salt and pepper
2 rashers bacon, cut into small pieces
1 tbsp capers
4 egg yolks

1. Cook the spaghetti in salted, boiling water. When cooked, drain, rinse in hot water and set aside to drain thoroughly.

2. Heat the milk and the cream in a saucepan. Season with salt and pepper.

3. Add the bacon and the capers and cook for 1 minute.

4. Add the drained spaghetti and cook until heated through completely.

5. Beat the egg yolks in a small bowl and then add them to the hot spaghetti. Remove the saucepan from the heat, stirring continuously with a wooden spoon, and serve.

TIME: Preparation takes about 5 minutes and cooking takes approximately 30 minutes.

SERVING IDEA: Sprinkle over a little grated Parmesan cheese just before serving.

WATCHPOINT: The spaghetti must be hot when the beaten egg yolk is added so that the egg cooks in the residual heat.

SPAGHETTI WITH TOMATO, SALAMI AND GREEN OLIVES

The sauce for this pasta is very quick to prepare, and the finished dish can be on the table in about 25 minutes.

SERVES 4

1 × 400g/14oz can crushed tomatoes
2 tbsps tomato purée
½ tbsp oregano
150g/5oz salami, sliced and shredded
200g/7oz green olives, pitted and chopped
Salt and pepper
225g/8oz spaghetti
2 tbsps olive oil
1 clove garlic, crushed
60g/2oz pecorino cheese, grated

1. Combine the crushed tomatoes, tomato purée, oregano, salami and olives in a saucepan and simmer for 15 minutes or until slightly thickened. Add salt and pepper to taste.

2. Meanwhile, cook the spaghetti in plenty of boiling salted water for 10 minutes, or until 'al dente'. Drain well.

3. Heat the olive oil and garlic in the pan used to cook the spaghetti. Add the spaghetti and pour the sauce over. Toss well. Serve immediately with the grated cheese sprinkled on top.

TIME: Preparation takes 15 minutes and cooking takes 15 minutes.

VARIATION: Use sliced pepperoni and black olives instead of the salami and green olives.

SERVING IDEA: Accompany with a green salad and crusty bread for a quick filling meal.

TORTIGLIONI ALLA PUTTANESCA

Serve this pasta dish with a crisp salad and some Italian bread.

SERVES 4

---

1 × 225g/8oz can plum tomatoes, drained
6-8 anchovy fillets
225g/8oz tortiglioni, spiral pasta
2 tbsps olive oil
2 cloves garlic, crushed
Pinch chilli powder
½ tsp basil
2 tbsps chopped parsley
60g/2oz black olives, pitted and chopped
Salt and pepper

1. Chop the tomatoes and remove the seeds, and chop the anchovies.

2. Cook the pasta in plenty of boiling salted water for 10 minutes, or until 'al dente'. Rinse in hot water, and drain. Pour into a warmed bowl.

3. Meanwhile, heat the oil in pan, add the garlic, chilli powder and basil, and cook for 1 minute.

4. Add the tomatoes, parsley, olives and anchovies, and cook for a few minutes.

5. Season with salt and pepper. Pour sauce over pasta, and mix together thoroughly. Serve immediately.

TIME: Preparation takes about 10 minutes and cooking takes 10-12 minutes.

VARIATION: Add a few capers to the sauce.

COOK'S TIP: Soaking the anchovies in a little milk before using will reduce their strong salty flavour.

FRESH PASTA WITH BOLOGNESE SAUCE

A rich, meaty sauce, cooked with white wine, carrots, onion and tomatoes.

SERVES 4

2 tbsps olive oil
1 carrot, finely diced
1 onion, finely diced
120ml/4 fl oz white wine
570g/1¼lbs minced beef
120ml/4 fl oz water
3 tomatoes, seeded and chopped
1 bay leaf
Salt and pepper
400g/14oz dried pasta shells
60g/2oz butter

1. Heat the olive oil in a casserole and sauté the carrot and onion until nicely browned.

2. Pour in the white wine and cook until the wine has completely evaporated.

3. Add the beef to the casserole and cook for 2 minutes stirring well to brown evenly.

4. Pour the water into the casserole, and add the tomatoes and the bay leaf. Season with salt and pepper, stir well and cook over a gentle heat for a further 30 minutes.

5. About half way through the cooking time for the sauce, set the pasta shells to cook in a pan of salted, boiling water until 'al dente', following manufacturers recommended cooking times. Rinse the pasta and allow it to drain.

6. Melt the butter and stir it into the pasta shells, then pour over the sauce and serve immediately. Serve piping hot.

TIME: Prepration takes about 15 minutes and cooking takes 40-50 minutes.

VARIATIONS: To make a slightly stronger flavoured sauce, add a bouquet garni made up of thyme, parsley and garlic to the sauce at Step 4.

COOK'S TIP: Allow the wine to evaporate completely, so that the sauce is flavoured by it and not affected by its acidity.

SICILIAN CANNELLONI

Cannelloni stuffed with meat, covered with slices of mozzarella and cooked in a chicken stock until crisp and golden on top.

SERVES 4

16 cannelloni tubes
60g/2oz butter
1 shallot, chopped
4 mushrooms, rinsed and chopped
2 slices ham, chopped
300g/11oz braising beef, minced
Salt and pepper
10 thin slices mozzarella cheese
120ml/4 fl oz chicken stock

1. Pre-cook the cannelloni in salted, boiling water for 1 minute. Set aside to drain.

2. Melt the butter in a saucepan or casserole and cook the shallot, mushrooms, ham and beef for about 10 minutes. Season with salt and pepper and set aside to cool.

3. When the stuffing is cool, fill the cannelloni, using a piping bag fitted with a plain nozzle, and place in a lightly-greased, ovenproof dish.

4. Place the slices of mozzarella over the cannelloni and then pour over the chicken stock.

5. Cook in a preheated oven at 190°C/375°F/Gas Mark 5 for about 15-25 minutes or until the dish is heated through and the top crisp and golden. Serve piping hot.

TIME: Preparation takes about 15 minutes, cooling takes about 15 minutes and cooking time is up to 25 minutes.

VARIATION: Use wild mushrooms, if available, in this cannelloni recipe.

COOK'S TIP: Once the cannelloni are cooked, spread them out onto a damp tea towel to prevent them from sticking together.

SPINACH LASAGNE

This lasagne contains a spinach sauce instead of the more usual meat sauce,
and is ideal for a vegetarian meal.

SERVES 4

8 sheets lasagne verdi

Spinach Sauce
60g/2oz butter or margarine
3 tbsps flour
120ml/4 fl oz milk
340g/12oz frozen spinach, thawed and
    finely chopped
Pinch of ground nutmeg
Salt and pepper

Parmesan Sauce
30g/1oz butter or margarine
2 tbsps flour
225ml/8 fl oz milk
45g/1½oz Parmesan cheese, grated
Salt

1. Heat the butter for the spinach sauce in a pan, stir in the flour and cook for 30 seconds. Draw off the heat, and gradually stir in the milk.

2. Return to the heat, and bring to the boil, stirring continuously. Cook for 3 minutes.

3. Add the spinach, nutmeg, and salt and pepper to taste. Set aside.

4. Cook the spinach lasagne in lots of boiling salted water for 10 minutes, or until tender. Rinse in cold water, and drain carefully. Dry on a clean cloth.

5. To make the parmesan sauce, heat the butter in pan and stir in the flour, cooking for 30 seconds. Remove from the heat, and stir in the milk.

6. Return to the heat, stirring continuously, until boiling. Continue stirring, and simmer for 3 minutes. Draw off the heat, and add two-thirds of the cheese, and salt to taste.

7. Grease an ovenproof baking dish. Line the base with a layer of lasagne, followed by some of the spinach mixture, and a layer of cheese sauce.

8. Repeat the process, finishing with a layer of lasagne and with a covering of cheese sauce. Sprinkle with the remaining cheese. Bake in an oven preheated to 200°C/400°F/Gas Mark 6, until golden on top. Serve immediately.

TIME: Preparation takes 15 minutes and cooking takes about 30 minutes.

COOK'S TIP: Use freshly grated Parmesan for the sauce, to get a good flavour.

PREPARATION: When the spinach thaws, squeeze it between two plates to remove any excess water.

PIZZA RUSTICA

This farmhouse pie is really a cross between quiche and pizza. Whichever you think it resembles most, there is no question that it is delicious.

SERVES 4-6

Pizza Dough
(see recipe for Pizza with Peppers, Olives
 and Anchovies)

Filling
Grated Parmesan cheese
120g/4oz prosciutto or Parma ham, sliced
2 tomatoes, skinned, seeded and roughly
 chopped
60g/2oz Mozzarella cheese, diced
1 tbsp chopped fresh parsley
1 tbsp chopped fresh basil
2 eggs, lightly beaten
75ml/5 tbsps double cream
60g/2oz Fontina cheese, finely grated
Pinch nutmeg
Salt and pepper

1. Prepare the dough as for the Pizza with Peppers, Olives and Anchovies. When the dough has doubled in bulk, knock it back and knead lightly. Flatten the dough into a circle or rectangle and roll out. Roll to a circle about 25cm/10-inches in diameter or a rectangle about 28×18cm/11-×7-inches.

2. Lightly oil the baking dish, place in the dough and press out with floured fingertips to form a raised edge on the sides of the dish.

3. Sprinkle the base of the dough with some of the Parmesan cheese and place on a layer of ham. Cover the ham with the chopped tomato. Mix the remaining ingredients together and pour over the tomato and ham.

4. Bake on the lowest shelf of an oven preheated to 190°C/375°F/Gas Mark 5, for about 35 minutes. The top of the pizza should be nicely browned and the edge of the dough should be golden when the pizza is ready. Serve hot.

TIME: Pizza dough takes 40 minutes to make, including rising time. Bake pizza for 35 minutes.

FREEZING: Pizzas can be prepared and frozen in their unbaked form. When cooking from frozen, allow an extra 10 minutes. Pizza dough bases may also be frozen unfilled. Allow to defrost before topping.

VARIATIONS: If Fontina cheese is not available, substitute Gruyère or Emmental. Vary the filling ingredients using different vegetables and meats as preferred.

HOME-MADE TAGLIATELLE WITH SUMMER SAUCE

Pasta making is not as difficult as you might think. It is well worth it, too, because home-made pasta is in a class by itself.

SERVES 4

Sauce

460g/1lb unpeeled tomatoes, seeded and cut into small dice

1 large green pepper, cut in small dice

1 onion, cut in small dice

1 tbsp chopped fresh basil

1 tbsp chopped fresh parsley

2 cloves garlic, crushed

140ml/¼ pint olive oil and vegetable oil mixed

Pasta Dough

120g/4oz plain flour

120g/4oz fine semolina

2 large eggs

2 tsps olive oil

Pinch salt

1. Combine all the sauce ingredients, mixing well. Cover and refrigerate overnight.

2. Place the flours in a mound on a work surface and make a well in the centre. Place the eggs, oil and salt in the centre of the well.

3. Using a fork, beat the ingredients in the centre to blend them and gradually incorporate the flour from the outside edge. The dough may also be mixed in a food processor.

4. When half the flour is incorporated, start kneading using the palms of the hands and not the fingers. This may also be done with a food processor. Cover the dough and leave it to rest for 15 minutes.

5. Divide the dough into quarters and roll out, thin enough to see through, with a rolling pin on a floured surface or use a pasta machine, dusting dough lightly with flour before rolling. If using a machine, follow the manufacturer's directions.

6. Allow the sheets of pasta to dry for about 10 minutes on a floured surface or tea towels. Cut the sheets into strips about 5mm/¼ inch wide by hand or machine, dusting lightly with flour while cutting.

7. Cook the pasta for 5-6 minutes in boiling salted water with a spoonful of oil. Drain the pasta and rinse under very hot water. Toss in a colander to drain excess water. Place the hot pasta in serving dish. Pour the cold sauce over and toss.

TIME: Preparation time takes about 30 minutes, cooking takes about 5-6 minutes.

WATCHPOINT: Pasta must remain very hot to balance the cold sauce.

SERVING IDEA: This basic pasta recipe can be used with other shapes of pasta such as lasagne, cannelloni, ravioli, farfalle (butterflies or bows) or cut into very fine noodles.

PENNE WITH HAM AND ASPARAGUS

The Italian word penne means quills, due to the diagonal cut on both ends of the pasta shapes.

SERVES 4

340g/12oz fresh asparagus
120g/4oz cooked ham
30g/1oz butter or margarine
280ml/½ pint double cream
225g/8oz penne

---

1. Using a swivel vegetable peeler, peel the sides of the asparagus spears starting about 5cm/2-inches from the top. Cut off the ends of the spears about 2.5cm/1-inch from the bottom.

2. Cut the ham into strips about 1.25cm/½-inch thick.

3. Bring a frying pan of water to the boil, adding a pinch of salt. Move the pan so it is half on and half off direct heat. Place in the asparagus spears so that the tips are off the heat. Cover the pan and bring back to the boil. Cook the asparagus spears for about 2 minutes. Drain and allow to cool.

4. Cut the asparagus into 5cm/1-inch lengths, leaving the tips whole.

5. Melt the butter in the frying pan and add the asparagus and ham. Cook briefly to evaporate the liquid, and add the cream. Bring to the boil and cook for about 5 minutes to thicken the cream.

6. Meanwhile, cook the pasta in boiling salted water with 1 tbsp oil for about 10-12 minutes.

7. Drain the pasta and rinse under hot water. Toss in a colander to drain and mix with the sauce. Serve with grated Parmesan cheese, if wished.

TIME: Pasta takes 10-12 minutes to cook. Sauce takes about 8 minutes to cook. Preparation takes about 20 minutes.

SERVING IDEA: May be served as a first course in smaller amounts.

SPIRALI WITH SPINACH AND BACON

Pasta doesn't have to have a sauce that cooks for hours. This whole dish takes about 15 minutes. True Italian "fast food"!

SERVES 4

225g/8oz fresh spinach, stalks removed
340g/12oz pasta spirals
3 tbsps olive oil
1 clove garlic, crushed
1 small onion, thinly sliced
1 small red pepper, finely sliced
1 small red or green chilli, seeded and
   finely sliced
90g/3oz rindless bacon finely diced
Salt and pepper

1. Wash the spinach leaves well, changing the water several times. Set aside to drain.

2. Cook the pasta in boiling salted water for about 10-12 minutes or until just tender.

3. Meanwhile roll up several of the spinach leaves into a cigar shape and then shred them finely. Repeat until all the spinach is shredded.

4. Just before the pasta is cooked heat the oil in a frying pan and add the garlic, onion, pepper, chilli and bacon. Fry for 2 minutes, add the spinach and fry for a further 2 minutes, stirring continuously. Season with salt and pepper.

5. Drain the pasta spirals and rinse under hot water, then toss in a colander to remove the excess water. Mix with the spinach and serve immediately.

TIME: Preparation takes about 20 minutes and cooking takes about 14 minutes.

PREPARATION: Wash spinach leaves in cold water to keep them crisp and change the water about three times to make sure all the grit is washed away.

WATCHPOINT: Handle chillies with care and wash hand well after chopping chillies as the juice tends to stick to the skin.

TUSCANY BEEF

Beef gently cooked in red wine and flavoured with rosemary and tomato makes a delicious casserole.

SERVES 4

900g/2lbs braising steak, cut into small cubes
Flour for dredging
3 tbsps olive oil
1 clove garlic, chopped
½ tsp chopped rosemary
520ml/18 fl oz red wine
2 tbsps tomato purée
Salt and pepper

1. Toss the meat cubes in the flour.

2. Heat the oil in a flameproof casserole, add the garlic, meat and rosemary. Fry on all sides until the meat is well browned.

3. Deglaze the casserole with the red wine and then pour in enough water to cover the meat.

4. Stir in the tomato purée, season with salt and pepper, cover and simmer gently for about 2 hours. Check the meat for tenderness and remove from the heat when cooked through. Serve hot.

TIME: Preparation takes about 10 minutes and cooking takes about 2 hours.

SERVING IDEA: Serve with plain boiled rice or steamed potatoes.

WATCHPOINT: Check the level of the liquid during cooking and add more water if necessary.

CHICKEN CACCIATORE

The name means Chicken the Hunter's Way, and that means the addition of mushrooms. Though not traditional, pasta is a good accompaniment.

SERVES 4-6

3 tbsps oil

120g/4oz mushrooms, quartered, if large

1.4kg/3lbs chicken joints, skinned if wished

1 onion

2 cloves garlic

140ml/¼ pint vermouth

1 tbsp white wine vinegar

140ml/¼ pint chicken stock

1 × 460g/1lb can tomatoes

1 tsp oregano

1 sprig fresh rosemary

Salt and pepper

60g/2oz black olives, pitted

2 tbsps chopped parlsey

1. Heat the oil in a heavy-based frying pan and cook the mushrooms for about 1-2 minutes. Remove them and set aside. Brown the chicken in the oil and transfer to an ovenproof casserole.

2. Chop the onion and garlic finely. Pour off all but 1 tbsp of the oil in the frying pan and reheat. Cook the onion and garlic until softened but not coloured.

3. Add the vermouth and vinegar and boil to reduce by half. Add the chicken stock, tomatoes, oregano, rosemary, salt and pepper. Break up the tomatoes and bring the sauce to the boil. Allow to cook for 2 minutes.

4. Pour the sauce over the chicken in the casserole, cover and cook at 180°C/350°F/Gas Mark 4 for about 1 hour.

5. Add mushrooms and olives during the last 5 minutes of cooking.

6. Remove the rosemary before serving and sprinkle with chopped parsley.

TIME: Preparation takes about 25-30 minutes, cooking takes about 1 hour 15 minutes.

COOK'S TIP: Pitted black olives are available in many delicatessens.

SERVING IDEA: Serve with spaghetti or pasta shapes and sprinkle with grated Parmesan cheese.

85

VEAL SCALOPPINE WITH PROSCIUTTO AND CHEESE

Veal is the meat used most often in Italian cooking. Good veal is tender and quick cooking, but expensive. Save this recipe for your next dinner party!

SERVES 4-8

8 veal escalopes
30g/1oz butter or margarine
1 clove garlic, crushed
8 slices prosciutto ham
3 tbsps sherry
140ml/¼ pint beef stock
1 sprig rosemary
8 slices mozzarella cheese
Salt and pepper

1. Pound the veal escalopes out thinly between two pieces of dampened greaseproof paper with a meat mallet or a rolling pin.

2. Melt the butter or margarine in a frying pan and add the veal and garlic. Quickly brown the veal on both sides.

3. Place a piece of prosciutto on top of each piece of veal and add the sherry, stock and sprig of rosemary to the pan. Cover the pan and cook the veal for about 8-10 minutes over a gentle heat or until done.

4. Remove the meat to a heatproof serving dish and top each piece of veal with a slice of cheese.

5. Bring the cooking liquid from the veal to the boil, season and allow to boil rapidly to reduce slightly.

6. Meanwhile, grill the veal to melt and brown the cheese. Remove the sprig of rosemary from the sauce and pour the sauce around the meat to serve.

TIME: Preparation takes about 15 minutes, cooking takes 15-20 minutes.

VARIATIONS: White wine may be substituted for the sherry, if wished. 1 tsp of tomato purée may be added to the sauce. Use chicken, turkey or pork instead of the veal.

PORK ROULADES WITH POLENTA

Polenta, either boiled or fried, is a staple dish in Italy as potatoes are elsewhere in the world.

SERVES 4-8

Polenta
1.7 litres/3 pints chicken stock
225g/8oz coarse yellow cornmeal
Salt and white pepper

Roulades
8 pork escalopes or steaks
8 slices Parma ham
4 large cup mushrooms
30g/4 tbsps grated Parmesan cheese
1 tbsp chopped fresh sage
Seasoned flour for dredging
60ml/4 tbsps olive oil
1 small onion, finely chopped
2 sticks celery, finely chopped
1 clove garlic, crushed
90ml/3 fl oz brown stock
140ml/¼ pint dry white wine
120g/4oz canned plum tomatoes, drained
    and juice reserved
1 tsp tomato purée
Salt and pepper
90ml/3 fl oz dry Marsala
Fresh sage leaves for garnish

1. Bring the chicken stock for the polenta to the boil in a large stock pot and start adding the cornmeal in a very slow, steady stream, stirring continuously. Add salt and pepper and continue cooking over very low heat, stirring frequently for about 55 minutes.

2. Flatten the pork escalopes or steaks until about 5mm/¼-inch thick and place a slice of Parma ham on top of each. Chop the mushrooms and divide among the pork escalopes, spooning on top of the ham slices. Sprinkle over the Parmesan cheese and the fresh sage.

3. Fold the sides of the pork escalopes into the centre to seal them, and roll up the pork like a Swiss roll starting from a short end. Secure each roll with a cocktail stick. Dredge each roulade in flour, shaking off the excess.

4. Heat the olive oil in a large frying pan and add the pork roulades, seam side down first. Cook on all sides until nicely browned. Remove the roulades and keep them warm.

5. Add the onion and celery to the oil in the pan and cook until lightly browned. Add the garlic and all the remaining ingredients except the Marsala and sage. Reserve the juice from the tomatoes for later use if necessary. Bring the sauce to the boil, breaking up the tomatoes.

6. Return the roulades to the pan, cover and cook over a moderate heat for about 15-20 minutes or until the pork is completely cooked. Add reserved tomato juice, as necessary, if the liquid is drying out.

7. When the pork is cooked, remove to a dish and keep it warm. Add the Marsala to the sauce and bring to the boil. Allow to boil for 5-10 minutes. The sauce may be puréed in a food processor and also sieved if wished.

8. To assemble the dish, spoon the polenta on a serving plate. Remove the cocktail sticks from the roulades and place on top of the polenta. Spoon the sauce over the meat and garnish the dish with fresh sage leaves.

LIVER VENEZIANA

As the name indicates, this recipe originated in Venice. The lemon juice offsets the rich taste of liver in this very famous Italian dish.

SERVES 4-6

Risotto

45g/1½oz butter or margarine

1 large onion, chopped

250g/9oz Italian risotto rice

60ml/4 tbsps dry white wine

Approximately 1.1 litres/2 pints boiling
    chicken stock

¼ tsp saffron

Salt and pepper

2 tbsps grated fresh Parmesan cheese

Liver

460g/1lb calves' or lambs' liver

Flour for dredging

30g/1oz butter or margarine

3 tbsps oil

3 onions, thinly sliced

Juice of ½ lemon

1 tbsp chopped parsley

Salt and pepper

1. Melt the butter for the risotto in a large pan, add the onion and cook until soft but not coloured, over a gentle heat.

2. Add the rice and cook for about a minute until the rice looks clear.

3. Add the wine, 140ml/¼ pint of the stock, saffron and seasoning. Stir well and bring to the boil. Lower the heat and cook gently, stirring frequently until the liquid has almost evaporated. Keep adding the stock in the same way, until the rice is tender. This will take about 40 minutes.

4. Meanwhile, skin the liver and cut out any large tubes.

5. Heat the butter or margarine and 1 tbsp oil in a large frying pan. Cook the onions until golden. Remove the onions from the pan to a plate.

6. Cut the liver into strips and toss in a sieve with the flour to coat.

7. Add more oil to the frying pan if necessary, heat, and add the liver. Cook, stirring constantly, for about 2 minutes.

8. Return the onions to the pan and add the lemon juice and parsley. Cook a further 2 minutes or until the liver is tender. Season with salt and pepper and serve with the risotto.

9. To finish the risotto, add the cheese and salt and pepper to taste when the liquid has evaporated and toss to melt the cheese.

TIME: Risotto takes about 50 minutes to prepare and cook. Liver takes about 4 minutes to cook.

WATCHPOINT: Liver and all offal needs short cooking or it will toughen.

PREPARATION: Tossing the liver and flour together in a sieve coats each piece of meat more evenly than can be done by hand.

TURKEY MARSALA

Marsala is a dessert wine from Sicily which also complements chicken, veal or turkey surprisingly well. It is traditional, but sherry will serve as a substitute if Marsala is unavailable.

SERVES 4

4 turkey breast fillets or escalopes
60g/2oz butter or margarine
1 clove garlic
4 canned anchovy fillets, soaked in milk
4 slices mozzarella cheese
Capers
2 tsps chopped marjoram
1 tbsp chopped parsley
3 tbsps Marsala
140ml/¼ pint double cream
Salt and pepper

1. If using turkey breast fillets, flatten them between two sheets of dampened grease-proof paper with a meat mallet or rolling pin.

2. Melt the butter in a frying pan and, when foaming, add the garlic and the turkey. Cook for a few minutes on each side until lightly browned, then remove them from the pan.

3. Drain the anchovy fillets and rinse them well. Dry on kitchen paper. Put a slice of cheese on top of each turkey fillet and arrange the anchovies and capers on top of each. Sprinkle with the chopped herbs and return the turkey to the pan.

4. Cook the turkey a further 5 minutes over a moderate heat, until the turkey is done and the cheese has melted. Remove to a serving dish and keep warm.

5. Return the pan to the heat and add the Marsala. Scrape the browned pan juices off the bottom and reduce the heat. Add the cream and whisk in well.

6. Lower the heat and simmer gently, uncovered, for a few minutes to thicken the sauce. Season the sauce with salt and pepper and spoon over the turkey fillets to serve.

TIME: Preparation takes about 25 minutes and cooking about 15 minutes.

WATCHPOINT: Turkey breast fillets are very lean so can dry out easily if over-cooked.

SERVING IDEA: Accompany the Turkey Marsala with new potatoes and lightly cooked courgettes.

ROAST PORK LOIN WITH ROSEMARY

An easy dish for entertaining, when you want to spend time with your guests and not in the kitchen.

SERVES 4

Rectangular strip of pork fat
2 cloves garlic, chopped
1 sprig rosemary, chopped
½ tsp coarse sea salt
Pepper
Few tarragon leaves
800g/1¾lbs boned pork loin
1 tbsp oil

1. Spread out the fat and sprinkle over the garlic, rosemary, sea salt, pepper and tarragon.

2. Place the loin, in a neat shape in the centre of the prepared fat and roll the fat around the meat. Secure with kitchen string.

3. Brush an ovenproof dish with oil, place in the pork loin and roast in an oven preheated to 200°C/400°F/Gas Mark 6, for 45-50 minutes or until the juices run clear, turning the pork over once, halfway through cooking.

4. Serve either hot or cold, cut into thick slices with the cooking juices spooned over.

TIME: Preparation takes about 15 minutes and cooking takes 45-50 minutes.

COOK'S TIP: Prepare the meat the day before cooking to allow the herbs and garlic to flavour the meat thoroughly.

SERVING IDEA: Accompany with new potatoes, carrots and broccoli.

TURKEY KEBABS

You don't have to buy a whole turkey for these! Small portions are now readily available at supermarkets and butchers.

SERVES 6

1.4kg/3lbs turkey meat
2 tsps chopped sage
1 sprig rosemary
Juice of 1 lemon
2 tbsps olive oil
Salt and pepper
120g/4oz rindless streaky bacon, bones
  removed
Whole sage leaves

---

1. Remove any bones from the turkey and cut the meat into even-sized pieces. Combine the chopped sage, rosemary, lemon juice, oil, and salt and pepper in a large bowl then add the turkey meat. Stir once or twice to coat evenly, cover and leave in the refrigerator overnight.

2. Cut the bacon rashers in half and stretch them by scraping with the blunt side of a knife blade. Wrap the bacon around some of the pieces of turkey. Leave other pieces of turkey unwrapped.

3. Thread the bacon-wrapped turkey, plain turkey and whole sage leaves onto skewers, alternating the ingredients.

4. Cook in a preheated 200°C/400°F/Gas Mark 6 oven for about 40 minutes. Alternatively, cook for 30 minutes and place the kebabs under a preheated grill for 10 minutes to crisp the bacon. Baste frequently with the marinade while cooking. Pour any remaining marinade and pan juices over the kebabs to serve.

TIME: Kebabs take about 20 minutes to assemble and need to marinate overnight. Cooking takes about 40 minutes.

VARIATION: Use chicken with chopped tarragon and whole bay leaves, if wished.

VEAL WITH MARSALA SAUCE

A smooth, slightly sweet sauce assures the success of this recipe.

SERVES 4

2 tbsps oil
1 large onion, finely sliced
900g/2lbs shoulder of veal, cut into cubes
60ml/2 fl oz almond-flavoured Marsala
1 sprig rosemary
Salt and pepper

1. Heat the oil in a large frying pan or a casserole and sauté the onion and meat until sealed all over and nicely browned.

2. Deglaze the pan with the Marsala and pour over sufficient water to completely cover the meat.

3. Add the rosemary to the pan, season with the salt and pepper and simmer gently for 45-50 minutes.

4. Remove from the heat and serve when the meat is cooked through and tender and the sauce has reduced and thickened.

TIME: Preparation takes about 10 minutes and cooking takes about 1 hour.

SERVING IDEA: Serve this dish with sauteed wild mushrooms and new potatoes or plain boiled rice.

WATCHPOINT: The exact cooking time will depend on the quality of the veal and the size of the cubes; check for tenderness during cooking and remove from the heat when done.

CASSATA

No sweet selection is complete without ice cream. The Italian kind is rich, creamy and justly famous.

SERVES 6-8

Almond Layer

2 eggs, separated
60g/2oz icing sugar
140ml/¼ pint double cream
½ tsp almond essence

Chocolate Layer

2 eggs, separated
60g/2oz icing sugar
140ml/¼ pint double cream
60g/2oz plain chocolate
2 tbsps cocoa
1½ tbsps water

Fruit Layer

280ml/½ pint double cream
1 egg white
60g/2oz icing sugar
2 tbsps maraschino or light rum
60g/2oz mixed glacé fruit
30g/1oz shelled, chopped pistachios

1. To prepare the almond layer, whisk egg whites until stiff peaks form, gradually beating in the icing sugar, a spoonful at a time. Lightly beat the egg yolks and fold in the whites. Whip the cream with the almond essence until soft peaks form and fold into the egg mixture. Lightly oil a 20cm/8-inch round cake tin. Pour in the almond layer mixture and smooth over the top. Cover with clingfilm and freeze until firm.

2. To prepare the chocolate layer, whisk the egg whites until stiff but not dry and gradually beat in the icing sugar. Whip the cream until soft and fold into the egg white mixture. Melt the chocolate in the top of a double boiler over simmering water. Remove it from the heat and stir in the egg yolks. Combine the cocoa and water and add to the chocolate mixture. Allow to cool and then fold into the egg white mixture. Spoon the chcolate layer over the almond layer and return, covered, to the freezer.

3. To make the rum fruit layer, whip the cream until soft peaks form. Whip the egg white until about the same consistency as cream. Gradually add the icing sugar, beating well after each addition. Combine the two mixtures, fold in the rum, fruit and nuts. Spread this mixture on top of the frozen chocolate layer, cover and freeze until firm.

4. To serve, loosen the cassata from around the edges of the pan with a small knife. Place a hot cloth around the pan for a few seconds to help loosen. Turn out onto a serving plate and cut into wedges to serve.

TIME: Preparation can take several hours, so that one ice cream layer can freeze before another is added.

RICOTTA PANCAKES WITH HONEY AND RAISIN SAUCE

These delicious pancakes are a real treat, and loved by all age groups.

SERVES 4

Filling
460g/1lb ricotta cheese
Grated rind of ½ lemon
2 tbsps raisins
1 tbsp chopped pine nuts

Pancakes
60g/2oz plain flour
Pinch salt
2 eggs
140ml/¼ pint water
1 tsp olive oil

Sauce
60ml/4 tbsps clear honey
Juice of ½ lemon
1 tbsp raisins
1 tbsp pine nuts
Twists of lemon, to decorate

1. For the filling: beat the cheese and the lemon rind until soft; mix in the raisins and pine nuts.

2. To make the pancakes, sift the flour with the salt. Break the eggs into a bowl and whisk. Gradually add the flour, whisking all the time, until the batter is smooth. Add the water and stir in well. Add the oil and mix.

3. Cover the bowl with a damp cloth and leave to stand in a cool place for 30 minutes.

4. Heat a crêpe pan or 18cm/7-inch frying pan. Lightly grease with a little melted butter.

5. Add a good tablespoon of batter to the centre of the pan and roll the pan to evenly coat the surface.

6. Cook until the pancake is brown on the underside. Loosen the edge with a pallette knife and flip over to brown the other side.

7. Repeat with the remaining batter to make 8 pancakes in all. Stack the pancakes, wrapped in a clean cloth and keep hot.

8. Put all the sauce ingredients into a small pan and warm through gently.

9. Divide the filling among the hot pancakes and either roll them up or fold them into triangles.

10. Arrange the pancakes on warm plates, spoon the sauce over the top and decorate with twists of lemon. Serve immediately.

TIME: Preparation takes 20 minutes plus 30 minutes standing time. Cooking takes about 20 minutes.

VARIATION: Substitute orange rind and juice for the lemon.

CARAMEL ORANGES

This is one of the classic Italian sweets. Vary the darkness of the caramel to suit your taste, but watch it carefully!

SERVES 4

4 large oranges
275g/10oz sugar
400ml/14 fl oz water
2 tbsps brandy or orange liqueur

1. Use a swivel vegetable peeler to peel thin strips from two of the oranges. Take off any white pith and cut the strips into very thin julienne strips with a sharp knife.

2. Place the julienne strips in a small saucepan, cover with water and bring to the boil.

3. Meanwhile, peel all the oranges with a serrated-edged knife. Cut the ends off first and then take the peel and pith off in very thin strips using a sawing motion. Cut the oranges horizontally into slices about 5mm/¼-inch thick. Drain the orange peel strips and leave to dry.

4. Combine the sugar and water in a heavy-based pan, reserving 60ml/2 fl oz of water for later use. Place the mixture over a medium heat until the sugar has dissolved. Add the drained orange peel strips to the pan.

5. Boil the syrup gently, uncovered, for about 10 minutes or until the orange strips are glazed. Remove the strips from the pan and place on a lightly oiled plate.

6. Return the pan to high heat and allow the syrup to boil, uncovered, until it turns a pale golden brown. Remove from the heat immediately and quickly add the extra water. Return to gentle heat and cook for a few minutes to dissolve hardened sugar. Remove the pan from the heat and allow to cool completely. Stir in the brandy.

7. Arrange the orange slices in a serving dish and pour over the cooled syrup. Pile the glazed orange strips on top and refrigerate for several hours, or overnight, before serving.

TIME: Preparation takes about 25 minutes, cooking takes about 10 minutes to parboil the orange strips and about 10-15 minutes to caramelize the syrup.

WATCHPOINT: Keep a close eye on the syrup as it is caramelizing. It can burn very quickly.

COOK'S TIP: All the white pith must be removed from the oranges and the orange strips or the whole dish will taste bitter.

CHESTNUT & ALMOND STUFFED PEACHES

A favourite sweet in Milan during the peach season.

SERVES 4-8

4 large ripe freestone peaches
280ml/½ pint dry white wine
2 tbsps brandy

Filling
60g/2oz plain chocolate
80g/2¾oz chestnut spread
1 egg yolk
1 tbsp peach liqueur or brandy
140ml/¼ pint double cream
1 tbsp ground almonds
4 amaretti or ratafia biscuits

1. Wash the peaches, peel them and cut them in half. Carefully remove the stones and place the peaches in a large bowl with the wine, brandy and enough water to cover them completely. Marinate for 1 hour.

2. Cut the chocolate into small pieces and melt in the top of a double boiler. Stir in the chestnut spread. Remove the chocolate from the heat and leave to cool for about 2 minutes, stirring frequently.

3. Beat in the egg yolk until well incorporated. Add the peach liqueur or brandy and stir well. Allow to cool.

4. Whip the cream and fold into the chocolate-chestnut mixture with the ground almonds. Allow to cool completely before using.

5. Remove the peaches from the marinade with a draining spoon and place them in serving dishes. Fill a piping bag, fitted with a large rosette nozzle, with the chocolate chestnut mixture.

6. Pipe out a large rosette of chocolate-chestnut mixture into the hollow of each peach half. Place a biscuit on top of each peach and serve chilled, with cream if wished.

TIME: Peaches take 1 hour to marinate, preparation takes about 40 minutes.

VARIATIONS: Nectarine halves may be used instead of peaches.

PREPARATION: Fresh peaches or nectarines must be placed in the wine and brandy mixture as soon as they are peeled or they will darken.

SERVING IDEA: Peach liqueur or brandy may be poured over each peach before filling, if wished.

ZUPPA INGLESE

This is Italy's tribute to trifle. The name means English soup, but the custard is rich and thick.

SERVES 6-8

2 tbsps cornflour
570ml/1 pint milk
2 eggs, lightly beaten
2 tbsps sugar
Grated rind of ½ lemon
Pinch nutmeg
460g/1lb ripe strawberries
16 sponge fingers
Amaretto liqueur
140ml/¼ pint double cream

1. Mix the cornflour with some of the milk. Beat the eggs, sugar, lemon rind and nutmeg together and pour in the remaining milk. Mix with the cornflour mixture in a heavy-based pan and stir over gentle heat until the mixture thickens and comes to the boil.

2. Allow to boil for 1 minute or until the mixture coats the back of a spoon. Place a sheet of greaseproof paper directly on top of the custard and allow it to cool slightly.

3. Save 8 even-sized strawberries for decoration and hull the remaining ones. Place half of the sponge fingers in the bottom of a large glass bowl and sprinkle with some amaretto.

4. Cut the strawberries in half and place a layer on top of the sponge fingers. Pour a layer of custard on top and repeat with the remaining sliced strawberries and sponge fingers. Top with another layer of custard and allow to cool completely.

5. Whip the cream and spread a thin layer over the top of the set custard. Pipe the remaining cream around the edge of the dish and decorate with the reserved strawberries. Serve chilled.

TIME: Preparation takes about 20 minutes, custard takes about 5 minutes to cook.

VARIATIONS: Decorate the top of the dessert with grated chocolate, toasted almonds or shelled pistachios in addition to, or instead of, the strawberries. Other fruit may be used, if wished.

ALMOND STUFFED FIGS

This simple dessert looks really sophisticated, and is the ideal finish to a dinner party.

SERVES 4

4 large ripe figs
30g/4 tbsps ground almonds
2 tbsps orange juice
2 tbsps finely chopped dried apricots
Wedges of ripe fig
Wedges of lime
Ground cinnamon

Sauce
60ml/4 tbsps cream
Finely grated rind of ½ orange

1. Make a cross cut in each fig, without cutting right down and through the base. Ease the four sections of each fig out, rather like a flower head.

2. Mix the ground almonds with the orange juice and chopped dried apricots; press into the centre of each fig.

3. For the sauce: mix the cream with the orange rind, and thin down with a little water.

4. Spoon a pool of orange flavoured cream onto each of 4 small plates; sit a stuffed fig in the centre of each one.

5. Decorate with wedges of fig and lime and a sprinkling of ground cinnamon.

TIME: Preparation takes about 20 minutes.

VARIATION: Use crème fraîche or greek yogurt for the sauce, and thin down with a little orange juice.

Index